AFRICAN WRITERS SERIES

208

Stubborn Hope

AFRICAN WRITERS SERIES

FOUNDING EDITOR Chinua Achebe

PETER ABRAHAMS
6 *Mine Boy*

CHINUA ACHEBE
1 *Things Fall Apart*
3 *No Longer at Ease*
16 *Arrow of God*
31 *A Man of the People*
100 *Girls at War**
120 *Beware Soul Brother*†

TEWFIK AL-HAKIM
117 *Fate of a Cockroach*‡

T. M. ALUKO
11 *One Man, One Matchet*
30 *One Man, One Wife*
32 *Kinsman and Foreman*
70 *Chief, the Honourable Minister*
130 *His Worshipful Majesty*

ELECHI AMADI
25 *The Concubine*
44 *The Great Ponds*
140 *Sunset in Biafra*§
210 *The Slave*

JARED ANGIRA
111 *Silent Voices*†

I. N. C. ANIEBO
148 *The Anonymity of Sacrifice*
206 *The Journey Within*

AYI KWEI ARMAH
43 *The Beautyful Ones Are Not Yet Born*
154 *Fragments*
155 *Why Are We So Blest?*
194 *The Healers*

BEDIAKO ASARE
59 *Rebel*

KOFI AWOONOR
108 *This Earth, My Brother*

FRANCIS BEBEY
86 *Agatha Moudio's Son*
205 *The Ashanti Doll*

MONGO BETI
13 *Mission to Kala*
77 *King Lazarus*
88 *The Poor Christ of Bomba*
181 *Perpetua and the Habit of Unhappiness*
214 *Remember Reuben*

OKOT p'BITEK
147 *The Horn of My Love*†
193 *Hare and Hornbill**

YAW M. BOATENG
186 *The Return*

DENNIS BRUTUS
46 *Letters to Martha*†
115 *A Simple Lust*†
208 *Stubborn Hope*†

AMILCAR CABRAL
198 *Speeches and Writing*

Keys to Signs
Novels are unmarked
*Short Stories
†Poetry
‡Plays
§Autobiography or Biography

SYL CHENEY-COKER
126 *Concerto for an Exile*†

DRISS CHRAIBI
79 *Heirs to the Past*

J. P. CLARK
50 *America, Their America*§

WILLIAM CONTON
12 *The African*

BERNARD B. DADIE
87 *Climbié*

DANIACHEW WORKU
125 *The Thirteenth Sun*

MODIKWE DIKOBE
124 *The Marabi Dance*

DAVID DIOP
174 *Hammer Blows*†

MBELLA SONNE DIPOKO
57 *Because of Women*
82 *A Few Nights and Days*
107 *Black and White in Love*†

AMU DJOLETO
41 *The Strange Man*
161 *Money Galore*

T. OBINKARAM ECHEWA
168 *The Land's Lord*

CYPRIAN EKWENSI
2 *Burning Grass*
5 *People of the City*
19 *Lokotown**
84 *Beautiful Feathers*
146 *Jagua Nana*
172 *Restless City and Christmas Gold**
185 *Survive the Peace*

OLAUDAH EQUIANO
10 *Equiano's Travels*§

MALICK FALL
144 *The Wound*

NURUDDIN FARAH
80 *From a Crooked Rib*
184 *A Naked Needle*

MUGO GATHERU
20 *Child of Two Worlds*§

NADINE GORDIMER
177 *Some Monday for Sure**

JOE DE GRAFT
166 *Beneath the Jazz and Brass*†

BESSIE HEAD
101 *Maru*
149 *A Question of Power*
182 *The Collector of Treasures**

LUIS BERNARDO HONWANA
60 *We Killed Mangy-Dog**

SONALLAH IBRAHIM
95 *The Smell of It**

YUSUF IDRIS
209 *The Cheapest Nights**

OBOTUNDE IJIMÈRE
18 *The Imprisonment of Obatala*‡

EDDIE IROH
189 *Forty-Eight Guns for the General*
213 *Toads of War*

AUBREY KACHINGWE
24 *No Easy Task*

SAMUEL KAHIGA
158 *The Girl from Abroad*

CHEIKH HAMIDOU KANE
119 *Ambiguous Adventure*

KENNETH KAUNDA
4 *Zambia Shall Be Free*§

LEGSON KAYIRA
162 *The Detainee*

A. W. KAYPER-MENSAH
157 *The Drummer in Our Time*†

ASARE KONADU
40 *A Woman in her Prime*
55 *Ordained by the Oracle*

MAZISI KUNENE
211 *Emperor Shaka the Great*

DURO LADIPO
65 *Three Yoruba Plays*‡

ALEX LA GUMA
35 *A Walk in the Night**
110 *In the Fog of the Seasons' End*
152 *The Stone Country*
212 *The Time of the Butcherbird*

DORIS LESSING
131 *The Grass is Singing*

TABAN LO LIYONG
69 *Fixions**
74 *Eating Chiefs**
90 *Franz Fanon's Uneven Ribs*†
116 *Another Nigger Dead*†

BONNIE LUBEGA
105 *The Outcasts*

YULISA AMADU MADDY
89 *Obasai*‡
137 *No Past, No Present, No Future*

NAGUIB MAHFOUZ
151 *Midaq Alley*
197 *Miramar*

NELSON MANDELA
123 *No Easy Walk to Freedom*§

RENE MARAN
135 *Batouala*

DAMBUDZO MARECHERA
207 *The House of Hunger**

ALI A. MAZRUI
97 *The Trial of Christopher Okigbo*

TOM MBOYA
81 *The Challenge of Nationhood (Speeches)*

S. O. MEZU
113 *Behind the Rising Sun*

HAM MUKASA
133 *Sir Apolo Kagwa Discovers Britain*§

DOMINIC MULAISHO
98 *The Tongue of the Dumb*
204 *The Smoke that Thunders*

CHARLES L. MUNGOSHI
170 *Waiting for the Rain*

JOHN MUNONYE
21 *The Only Son*
45 *Obi*
94 *Oil Man of Obange*
121 *A Wreath for the Maidens*
153 *A Dancer of Fortune*
195 *Bridge to a Wedding*

MARTHA MVUNGI
159 *Three Solid Stones**

MEJA MWANGI
143 *Kill Me Quick*
145 *Carcase for Hounds*
176 *Going Down River Road*

GEORGE SIMEON MWASE
160 *Strike a Blow and Die*§

NGUGI WA THIONG'O
7 *Weep Not Child*
17 *The River Between*
36 *A Grain of Wheat*
51 *The Black Hermit*‡
150 *Secret Lives**
188 *Petals of Blood*
200 *Devil on the Cross*

NGUGI & MICERE MUGO
191 *The Trial of Dedan Kimathi*‡

REBEKA NJAU
203 *Ripples in the Pool*

ARTHUR NORTJE
141 *Dead Roots*†

NKEM NWANKWO
67 *Danda*
173 *My Mercedes is Bigger Than Yours*

FLORA NWAPA
26 *Efuru*
56 *Idu*

ONUORA NZEKWU
85 *Wand of Noble Wood*
91 *Blade Among the Boys*

OGINGA ODINGA
38 *Not Yet Uhuru*§

GABRIEL OKARA
68 *The Voice*
183 *The Fisherman's Invocation*†

CHRISTOPHER OKIGBO
62 *Labyrinths*†

KOLE OMOTOSO
102 *The Edifice*
122 *The Combat*

SEMBENE OUSMANE
63 *God's Bits of Wood*
92 *The Money-Order* with *White Genesis*
142 *Tribal Scars**
175 *Xala*

YAMBO OUOLOGUEM
99 *Bound to Violence*

MARTIN OWUSU
138 *The Sudden Return*‡

FERDINAND OYONO
29 *Houseboy*
39 *The Old Man and the Medal*

PETER K. PALANGYO
53 *Dying in the Sun*

SOL T. PLAATJE
201 *Mhudi*

R. L. PETENI
178 *Hill of Fools*

LENRIE PETERS
22 *The Second Round*
37 *Satellites*†
103 *Katchikali*†

JEAN-JOSEPH RABEARIVELO
167 *Translations from the Night*†

MUKOTANI RUGYENDO
187 *The Barbed Wire & Other Plays*‡

MWANGI RUHENI
139 *The Future Leaders*
156 *The Minister's Daughter*

TAYEB SALIH
47 *The Wedding of Zein**
66 *Season of Migration to the North*

STANLAKE SAMKANGE
33 *On Trial for my Country*
169 *The Mourned One*
190 *Year of the Uprising*

WILLIAMS SASSINE
199 *Wirriyamu*

KOBINA SEYKI
136 *The Blinkards*‡

SAHLE SELLASSIE
52 *The Afersata*
163 *Warrior King*

FRANCIS SELORMEY
27 *The Narrow Path*

L. S. SENGHOR
71 *Nocturnes*†
180 *Prose and Poetry*

ROBERT SERUMAGA
54 *Return to the Shadows*

WOLE SOYINKA
76 *The Interpreters*

TCHICAYA U TAM'SI
72 *Selected Poems*†

CAN THEMBA
104 *The Will to Die**

REMS NNA UMEASIEGBU
61 *The Way We Lived**

LAWRENCE VAMBE
112 *An Ill-Fated People*§

J. L. VIEIRA
202 *The Real Life of Domingos Xavier*

D. M. ZWELONKE
128 *Robben Island*

COLLECTIONS OF STORIES AND PROSE
9 *Modern African Prose*
14 *Quartet* By Richard Rive, Alex La Guma, Alf Wannenburgh and James Matthews
15 *Origin East Africa*
23 *The Origin of Life and Deat[h]*
48 *Not Even God is Ripe Enough*
58 *Political Spider*
73 *North African Writing*
75 *Myths and Legends of the Swahili*
83 *Myths and Legends of the Congo*
109 *Onitsha Market Literature*
118 *Amadu's Bundle* Malum Amadu
132 *Two Centuries of African English*
196 *Egyptian Short Stories*

ANTHOLOGIES OF POETRY
8 *A Book of African Verse*
42 *Messages: Poems from Ghana*
64 *Seven South African Poets*
93 *A Choice of Flowers*
96 *Poems from East Africa*
106 *French African Verse*
129 *Igbo Traditional Verse*
164 *Black Poets in South Africa*
171 *Poems of Black Africa*
192 *Anthology of Swahili Poetry*

COLLECTIONS OF PLAYS
28 *Short East African Plays*
34 *Ten One-Act Plays*
78 *Short African Plays*
114 *Five African Plays*
127 *Nine African Plays for Radio*
134 *African Theatre*
165 *African Plays for Playing 1*
179 *African Plays for Playing 2*

STUBBORN HOPE

New poems and selections from
China Poems and *Strains*

DENNIS BRUTUS

LONDON
HEINEMANN
IBADAN · NAIROBI · LUSAKA

Heinemann Educational Books Ltd
48 Charles Street, London W1X 8AH
P.M.B. 5205 Ibadan · P.O. Box 45314 Nairobi
P.O. Box 3966 Lusaka

EDINBURGH MELBOURNE TORONTO AUCKLAND SINGAPORE
HONG KONG KUALA LUMPUR NEW DELHI KINGSTON

ISBN 0 435 90208 3

Stubborn Hope first published 1978

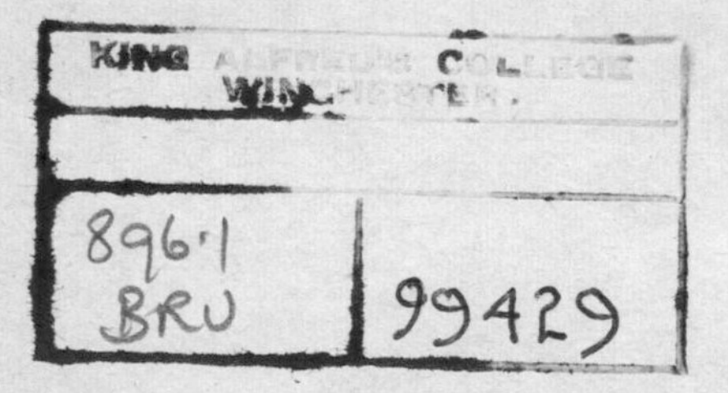

Set in 11 on 12pt Souvenir
Printed in Great Britain by
Cox & Wyman Ltd., London, Fakenham and Reading.

Table of Contents

Poems Collected for this Edition:

Note

Of all the poems collected for this edition, those on pages 1 to 24 were written in South Africa, as were those on pages 52-72, with the exception of *Snarling, the great beast hurls through the dark; In Teheran; I remember the simple practicality of your reminiscences; Having fled, I display a fugitive's jealousy* and *In Memoriam: I.A.H.*

Words for Farewell

Rusted idioms ring anew
As bell-buoys speak with pristine tongue
Navy and heaving the sea becomes
And footprints shrink their imprint due

Here, my heart at sea, my dear
I mouth the gaunt eroded words
and find them sea-changed into sense
that surges in my caverned ear

Those hinted bulks that slip astern
Hooting across the spangled wastes
Are part of all I seek to say
Spray-salt, as I move away.

Inscription for a copy of Road to Ghana *by Alfred Hutchinson*

Well, we have caged our bird
and he has sung for us
as sweet a song as any heard—
time now, we freed our bird.

Skylark or nightingale
who cares beyond delight?
For all birds fly a vagrant trail
and the music cannot stale.

Out of the blue he dips
unearned and unenslaved
to brush with his wing our wondering lips
and break our fingertips.

All life the timeless song
will pierce the crash of life
and if I call my bird for long
"Phoenix" will I do wrong?

In this country

In this country;
In this air;
Where these trees grow;

Where clear air flows
Before, behind, above
And through the throat,
Flows a cool and crystal stream
To where the milkwhite domes
In an all-embracing curve

In this country,
In this air,
Where these trees grow

Poised and moving
As a flame intruding
Projects through rings of encircling dark,

Where sweet air flows,
And the slim trees grow,
In this country
Festers hate in fetid wounds
Infection floats on fluid air
Anger roars in the placid night
And the dark is drizzled with our tears.

The wide grey cloud of sky

The wide grey cloud of sky
the smoke-drab world of after-rain
And this one burst of sun
shafting down to turn my private world
to crystal and to flame.
Such joy—sudden—bright as a flag unfurled
I never thought to see again
after our love was done.
But see, but see
There are still other worlds
than our special private buried world.

Strelitzias

Strelitzias,
phoenixes

in the late level afternoon light,
take flight,
exquisitely.

I know now it was vain to seek

I know now it was in vain to seek
to hold you, or any part of you:
know too I have the finest gift
—untarnishable and secure:
in secret places of my self
is an assurance and a strength
I drew from the warmth you gave
and all my range of thought and feeling
is wider, stronger and more free
from mere touching of your spirit's hem

Janus

One face speaks emollient words
while one contrives my mutilation
One spews homeword hypocritic turds
the other overseas upbraids hypocritic nations

One furrows anxiously for birds
while one condones a man's castration

But where will they look when anger makes its ring
or draws the noose of vengeful suffering?

For My Sons & Daughters

Memory of me will be a process
of conscious and unconscious exorcism;
not to condemn me, you will need
forgetfulness of all my derelictions,
and kindness will be only yours
if you insist on clinging steadfastly
to some few small exaggerated symbols—
"This much he cared," or "Thus he did"
and "If he could, he would have done much more."

This I can understand, for my affection
enables me to penetrate the decades and your minds
and now I seek no mitigation—
would even welcome some few words of scorn;
but it might help if, reading this,
in after adult bitter years,
you are enabled then to say: "He really cared then?"
"Really cared?" "Our fictions have some substance then!"

I will not ask you then to add what I do now:
my loneliness; my failures; my amalgam wish to serve:
my continental sense of sorrow drove me to work
and at times I hoped to shape your better world.

This soft small rain, falling down

This soft small rain, falling down
makes no demands on our attention,
is murmurless and has no power
to penetrate and force protection;
this is a shy tug at shirt or skirt,
a whisper at the cheek or ear:
so a stray love, a humble tenderness
might proffer its caress and so achieve
a small perfection of its own.

The green days of late summer

The green days of late summer
with lascivious allure
thrust lust into my tenderness—
the spouse plays paramour!

What wonder then that Autumn
falls rapaciously on trees—
those voluptuous Sabinians
who incite such lecheries?

I have not, out of love, cursed you yet

I have not, out of love, cursed you yet,
though anger and impatience often rock me;
nor have my clawed hands dug in you
with imprecations of obscene abuse,
but know that frenzies may yet come:
remember then that my frustrated tenderness
bursts out in violence of suppressed love,
my fury out of unattended love.

The price, the name, are of no account

The price, the name, are of no account
so the thing recalls your presence.

Where there are female things I ferret
blindly hoping for some trace of you
who were all the women in the world.

And so, in a single gulping sniff
I confirm that this indeed recalls you
and instantaneously summon you fleshed
and smiling, pink, alight with love

By this perfume, confirmed, confirm
the meaning of its sweet remembrance.

You tested my love for my real true love

You tested my love for my real true love
and such a test the mediaevals could not dream:
having relinquished you for my true love
I know my love can endure, resist all things—
even as storms and footprints scar her ravaged face
and leave her dearness still unmarred.

Winter seeps from the concrete

Winter seeps from the concrete
and puddles around my knees
and all day long in my spirit
I hear the drip drip of rain

When will you come, my love
and when will you come again?

I see the cold-scorched edges
of the drear dispirited trees,
leaves drift in limp surrender
from boughs weighed down by rain

When will you come, my love
and when will you come again?

My blood exhales its fire
in a weariness like age
and the heart dulls at the edges
like stones worn smooth by rain

When will you come, my love
and when will you come again?

Chill encircles my marrow,
hope embers in cold ash
and patient waiting narrows
to a single thread like pain

When will you come, my love
and when will you come again?

The slim girl–grace of early autumn trees

The slim girl–grace of early autumn trees
has an individual message too;
scatters of gaudy yellow–gold confetti
amid the febrile glitter of hectic green
confer, deceptively, the festiveness of brides:

thus the consumptive's frantic gaiety
before pneumonia's sudden puncturing,
and thus with an autumnal pang I see
the springing buoyance of my urgent stride
is galvanised by secret rottings at the root.

When they deprive me of the evenings

When they deprive me of the evenings
how shall I speak my inexpressible grief?

Think of the night–air, sweet with dew and stars
the moon a molten ingot's spilling–splash
plaqued on the night's glassed–ocean floor,
the elegance of lamp–lit autumn oaks
preening in accidental man-made grace
and this rat–ceilinged hovel on my head.

When I am prisoned from my evenings
how shall I word my inarticulable woe?

I shall curl to the tight knot of a shrivelled worm
or angularly bundled like a mangy cat
huddle against myself for warmth
or grub among leaf–litter of my autumn years
rustling foregone endearments in my throat
and seeking easement in remembered tenderness

but how shall I mouth my unencompassable woe
and how shall I be consoled?

The beauty of this single tree

The beauty of this single tree
obedient to the season's icebound laws
and stoic under winter's knouts,
the fragile pathos of its tattered rags
still steadfastly unfurled
like unsurrendered flags
of some long-lost and gallant cause
a fecund and diurnal logic
conceived and brought about:

and this, this beauty of a single tree
redeems my lunatic
and stone and iron world.

I remembered in the tranquil Sunday afternoon

I remembered in the tranquil Sunday afternoon,
looking out on the villas and plazas,
how friend Frederico Lorca died

from the prison window I could see
a roccoco church and a square with waving grass
and beyond, the gaudy facade of the bullring

Overhead the hard bright blue of the sky
compounded of tropic light and the salt air of the sea
and palms waved amid tropic profusion of flowers

hibiscus and wisteria especially
and when we rode there wafted into the prison truck
a scent of syringa and wild orange

and something that might have been frangipani
and in the gathering afternoon that Sunday
I remembered how the poet Lorca died.

It's fun *

It's fun
in the sun
and cool
in the pool
with pleasant shadows
to hide away
and I never know need

with a regular feed
at special times every day

But oh to be free
in the wide open sea
roaming the ocean meadows
or to laze in the bay
and gambol all day

To be free, to be free, to be free!

* For Julian who asked for a dolphin poem

Endurance is the ultimate virtue

Endurance is the ultimate virtue
—more, the essential thread
on which existence is strung
when one is stripped to nothing else
and not to endure is to end in despair.

For us, only the barrennest of existences

For us, only the barrennest of existences
in a Siberia of avarice:

vainly one's mind traverses the festivities,
seeks for one hillock on the sterile plain

so one returns to the recognition:
nothing for us is offered, nothing gained.

Taut, with lean care–haunted face

Taut, with lean care–haunted face
gaunt and thrusting as a whippet's
I scent the dank cold air of time,
throat–bared and vulnerable
and almost desperate in my searchingness.

What do they expect from me?

What do they expect from me?
and what do they expect me to do?
I cannot play heroic parts
and will not posture for their delectation
and when I urge—
circumspectly enough, I am sure—
them to pursue the lines
that brought me where I am
they shrink, or find excuse.
Anyway, I know it will not be done.

What could be dearer

What could be dearer
than this hunger
that seeks to devour
the laggard hour
merely to stand within the aura
of the loved–one's presence?

When will my heart

When will my heart
ever again sing?
or speak of something,
find some rare delight?

Where is the lyric impulse
Where the gift
and where the will
to fashion something beautiful?

A chance impulse

A chance impulse,
chance allusion,
and if the will be blessed
by the beneficent will,
enterprise flourishes,
endeavour comes to flower.

Blurs of colour, strands of scent

Blurs of colour, strands of scent
return with the transience of the ending year:
one wonders what unknown delights
waited: and recalls the known and dear.

There are times (1)

There are times
when the pattern of events
in the physical world
falls into such a pleasing design
that I dare be convinced
that they have been arranged
by the tender cajoling hands
of a near–divine maternal graciousness

When will I return

When will I return
to the tightly organised
complexly structured
image and expression
rich in flying tangential associations
that buttress, ore–vein or embroider
and sing with a complexity of feeling
and richness of expression
butterfly–fluttery in the belly
mosquito-swarming around the head
and thrumming like the windharps of the forest
in the emotional branches of mind and nerves.

Grace is winged and capable of flight

Grace is winged and capable of flight
and mercy over–exercised
hardens to condemnation

And so a time must come
when forgiveness is a mistake
and justice is expressed in punishment

Land that I love, now must I ask

Land that I love, now must I ask
dare I discard the diurnal mask
of feeling, the protective husk
of manufactured feeling hiding hurt
Now that you show your secret hues
and hint in flickering tints your permanent heart
glimmering and tender in the luminous dark
your exposed loveliness dissolving away my fear
Now must I wonder if I dare,
dare I discard my quotidian mask?

It is time I said a word

It is time I said a word
and shattered my too tactful silence
which glasses off my erstwhile friends
from injury:

how I am shamed
by those who pass me by
with just that break in stride
which shows a momentary hesitation!

And how my heart heels
averting itself
from anger, hurt, contempt
when some slink by
pretending ignorance
of my presence!

And those who do not dare to write
or send the simplest word
of seasonal conventional greeting
—hugging close some not–so–wonderfully

feathered nest
and turning to me
only that side of them
that has been frozen to obliviousness

It is understandable that some should stay away
out of uncertaintly of the exact provisions of the law
and rumour gives rise to the grossest exaggerations
but those who cower away
out of fear to be involved.....

Dear wonderful woman

Dear wonderful woman
mother and friend and guide
rest easy now from all the strain
the courageous grasping of our jagged life
or better still—for this I desire
and dare to hope already your reward—
rejoice in bliss to crown your work
that insulates you from our present woe

Most gracious exemplar

Most gracious exemplar
weaving your virutes with a modesty
that made them seem unpresent
and waging with a womanly lack of emphasis
tenacious battle with a world
of multiple injustice and evil—
whoever had the blessing of a dearer guide
and yet so little cared–for, little loved?

Afterglow

Having done this
I can do more:

having taken,
given,
possessed,
imposed my being
through impassioned fusing will

so much more of the world
awaits my will—
the aftermath of this act.

Let the shiphorns hoot and blare

Let the shiphorns hoot and blare
at the passing of the year
and tipsy revellers klaxon their merriment
in their complacent fug

But oh may we hope that some will turn
to those who toss on coir mats amid stone–walls
and writhe their restless loneliness

Once you spoke

Once you spoke
in a dear moving phrase
of my patient endurance:

Who would have thought
I should need it now for you,
or you find it intolerable?

How are the shoots of affection withered at the root?

How are the shoots of affection withered at the root?
What lops the tendrils that reach out
and what blights the tender feeling buds?

All that I dreamed—and doubtless you—
and that we fondly hoped and planned
how was it poisoned and with what?

Blighted withered are the leaves
a foul miasma breathes
and rheumy exudations seep
and a wormwood bitterness surrounds

How are the shoots of affection withered!

There are times (2)

There are times
when our repudiation of ourselves
is so complete
the acceptance of our corruption
so absolute
the thrust of our concupiscent propensities
so unarguable
that capitulation,
surrender
—nay more!
the embrace of despair
is almost final

And then
our only consolation
relief
must be found outside ourselves

in the nature of God
and *his* desires

And one remembers Augustine:
God made us for himself
and we desire him
because it is *his* desire
(It is by clinging to the nature of God
that we escape despair
in our own nature).

Hell is just stupidity

Hell is just stupidity
and blundering
and crassness;

a gross assault
on the sensitivities
of the least:

it is the brutal indifference
to the gentle and the good
that earns hell

and hell is just a place
of bruising assault on one's self
in a willed deliberate stupidity

A Comparative Peace

Flesh-yielding
heart-surrender
is only part of it
is only a comparative peace

One requires
more
an intellectual acceptance
assent
the erasure of sharp memories
whose cicatrices leave stiff tissue
a reluctant unbending

so
in the recesses of the heart
discontent stirs

one knows
only an unquiet ease
only a comparative peace.

It is without the overtones

It is without the overtones
of wry cynicism
—as I know you will understand—
that I say
I raise my eyes
to the Abergavenny hills
and find there some small easement

One guesses his occupation

One guesses his occupation:
satchel and suit and pompous hat
and the sheen of spurious smartness

What does he do and what is his polish?
Then past the smoothness thrusts the truth:

This is the upholder of the law
(which is far from being the same as justice)
and so there is dignity and self-respect
and callous boots to trample decencies

but this is not what rouses fear and queasiness:
it is the sense of robot power with far beyond
the deeper sense of power arbitrarily unleashed
and this is the corruption at the vitals:
the glazed ripeness of rotten fruit

An exquisite painful pleasure

An exquisite painful pleasure,
as of sore muscles in a hot
bath after day's sport;
fingering the shrinking edges of a healing wound;
an agonised enriching catharsis in Lear or Oedipus;
the calculated abandon of a gaudy night.

Why shouldn't it be true

Why shouldn't it be true?
absolutely true
for some at least?

doesn't acceptance
of a provident omniscience
embrace just this?

that for each of us
there is a perfectly matched person
the fulfillment of our impulse to love?

In this world

In this world
and confronting in my thought
the world I expect to confront

I am all that I am
and more than I am
and so much less than I am

as I remember
and discover—re-discover
sadly, sickly, impotently.

Beyond sharp control

Beyond sharp control
lies phoenix paper packaging
at first exposed,
now gradually enclosed
and all of it symbolical;
like the questions:
tell me did your wife know?
and does she trust you now?

I would not be thought less than a man

I would not be thought less than a man
in feeling or understanding
and so must balance my revulsion
with its implied offence
to those to whom it is affliction
or fulfillment of a richly personal need,
and so I place on record facts I know

which build a wholly other world—
the hints of tenderness and passion
not blazoned forth as the false and insincere
the genuine concern and anxiousness
between two men whom sexual bonds had linked:
not all of it was evil it must seem
(we except of course, seduction, outrage, rape)
or some of it had graces that I know not of

Stubborn Hope

Endurance is a passive quality,
transforms nothing, contests nothing
can change no state to something better
and is worthy of no high esteem;
and so it seems to me my own persistence
deserves, if not contempt, impatience.

Yet somewhere lingers the stubborn hope
thus to endure can be a kind of fight,
preserve some value, assert some faith
and even have a kind of worth.

I will be the world's troubadour

I will be the world's troubadour
if not my country's

Knight-erranting
jousting up and down
with justice for my theme

weapons as I find them
and a world-wide scatter of foes

Being what I am
a compound of speech and thoughts and song

and girded by indignation
and accoutred with some undeniable scars
surely I may be
this cavalier?

The mesh of circumstance

The mesh of circumstance
nets me in its metal gauge
against which I lacerate myself
while the moth-mind flutters, flutters
vainly prying for escape
bearing the scoring rebuffs
that flake the shivering cerebrum like scales

For them Burness Street is a familiar entity

For them Burness Street is a familiar entity,
it lies whole, like a snake,
in the landscape of their minds
with its length and intersections
its trees and pavements, corners, shops
drains and gutters, curbs and slopes:

but for me, apart from its known beginning-point
and the dim extensions this implies
it came to me, twice, as a sudden surprise
both in its middle, crossing a known tract
and at its sudden tree-marked end
with the double-storeyed red-painted house
the grassy verge and friendly shutters
and the lovely laughing courteous girl
with shoulder-bobbed hair and the regular lines

that catch the near-perfect beauty of symmetry—
and, afterwards the moving story
of her secret patient waiting forbidden love.

For them, all South End is the familiar map
of their existence, all their growth and lives
though for me it is mere knowledge, mere report:
yet even I can sorrow, knowing their loss
their uprooting from their homely paradise
and all their yearnings and their sense of loss.

(A note on the effect of the Group Areas Act. South End
is an area from which the non-whites are being forced
to move as a result of this Act.)

I must speak

I must speak
(this is my desire)
in the channels of your ear
in your silent moments,
or when your heart answers
and, seeking words,
hears echoes rise
unbidden
in the tunnels of the mind

I must speak
so plangently
(this is my desire)
in the channels of your ear
that in your silent moments
my words will reverberate:

or when your heart answers
some strong assertion of the truth
in blood, or action or belief and seeks for words
let then my echoes rise
unbidden
in the tunnels of your mind.

I come and go

I come and go
a pilgrim
grubbily unkempt
stubbornly cheerful
defiantly whistling hope
and grubbing for crumbs of success
out of all near-defeats

I shuffle through the waiting rooms
and the air-terminals of the world
imposing and importuning
while the politely courteous
acquaintances
co-operate
help arrange my departures
without any pang of greeting

I work my stubborn difficult unrewarding will
obtusely addleheaded clumsy:
some few things happen
and I plod or shuffle or amble
wracked with anguished frustrate hunger
and go on.

Here, of the things I mark

Here, of the things I mark
I note a recurring hunger for the sun

—but this is not homesickness,
the exile's patriate thirst:

At home, in prison, under house-arrest
the self-same *smagting*° bit me

now is the same as then
and here I live as if still there.

*Afrikaans for yearning.

I willed for myself an oblivious rush

I willed for myself an oblivious rush
that shielded me from a sense of loss
and blinkered myself with pre-empting chores
that cloaked me from a stranger's land:

Now, for a while, I have opened myself
and wonder if it is not unwise.

Lovers whose limbs were marbled

Lovers whose limbs were marbled
by this Adriatic moon
or Romans stepping down to board
above this mighty muscled surge
or flail through waves along a silver road
the sun poured from an accessible horizon,
what dreams you might not have
here where the world is splendid as a dream
and from these shores confers upon a stubborn world
the aura and the body of romance.

And here, in understanding just how dreams are born
I grant myself the license and the joy of dreams,
muse greatly, think of love, and hope, and dream

If this life is all we have

If this life is all we have
if in fact it is all we shall know
as indeed may be most probable
and if, as is reasonably certain
we shall have no more on earth
then it is wrong to lament—

wrong to wish for the end of life
wrong to feel one must drag somehow through
and surely one must do whatever one can
fill each day with as much as can be done
while we live, we must fill each day with living
and do each day as much as we can
of what seems to us worthwhile:
all that is good, as we understand it
all that stirs us with a sense of joy
and this we must do each day as much as we can
while we are living
since this may be the only life
and certainly the only one we shall know here
it is sensible to make it full and alive
and rich and satisfying
and filled with all that seems to us good,
and that seems enduring and brings joy
all that seems virtuous
all that seems alive.

English Autumn

The stubborn endurance of November rose

Leaves pock the grass
on soggy lawns
where recalcitrant copper-beeches strip.

The light, the air
in singing clearness of rain-burnished air

and then the tenderness
when mistsoft-blue shadows
the middle distance trees
at dusk.

In this dampness
the rotting vegetation
the febrile brilliance of day
the twilight autumn melancholy
at bottom
lies the toughness of cold stone
the enduringness of underground sinewy roots.

In the afternoon

In the afternoon
before the sunset
the Lagos air
comes sweet and cool
green and leafy
through the tired day
and around my temples.

I love to shamble through the dusk

I love to shamble through the dusk
trailing my feet in shards and cinders of old dust,
greeting the frizzled petals on the vines,
sniffing for perfumes half-decayed, half-lingering
in my mind—
where the old psychic charges, lacking goals or breadth
explode in missile longings, hurtling for a blind
and shattering destructive death.

On torn ragged feet

On torn ragged feet
trailing grimy bandages
with bare thin legs
I puttered around the prison yard awhile
while politicos learning of me gaped
wondering how they had managed to make of me
a thing
of bruises, rags, contempt and mockery.

In time things grew better.

For a while I was the tattooed lady of the prison

For a while I was the tattooed lady of the prison
and warders would come to our section and get me to strip
and stare and whistle in mingled pleasure and horror
at the great purple bruise that ran from my neck down
my back,
from my neck to my thighs in a purple mass

What was I then?
mute enduring reproach
heroic endurer
Christianly hero
submissive ass?
What was I then
that I cannot now image
cannot now judge?

There was a time when the only worth

There was a time when the only worth
was other men—
their saleable value;
one felt the steady venom
in the gaze of another shackled
and knew the relief of escaping,
and in another day bowed down
accepting this ignominious ultimate:

war did not make captors—
for captors one made war:
and captives were the purpose of the war:

so, for alien almost-humans
we made hunted beasts of humans.
Till time brings its reverses.

Sherds

Sherds
This is the image that coheres my world
to a single shape, single sharp edge

and I see them in my mind
the broken brittle edges,
brick-red like broken tiles
stuck in the moist black earth
to border an unkempt garden

sherds,
potsherds
—with the images of beetles' empty cases
thin, sharp-edged and brittle
slim black crackling blades—
Sherds!

—of bucolics
wrapped in hairy skin-robes
grouped with gnarled horny feet
around an open pastoral fire—
twigsmoke, logs and cooking pots

—of lugubrious Job
with his egregious comforters
scraping the scabs
and puncturing the pustulent excrescences
of his inflicted loathsomeness

Sherds:
there are the images
to catch the world senses first apperceive
and this the image that I seize upon
when speaking my habitual commentary
while picking my judicious passage through the world.

It was a sherded world I entered

It was a sherded world I entered:
of broken bottles, rusty tins and split rooftiles:
the littered earth was full of menace
with jagged edges waiting the naked feet:
holes, trenches, ditches were scattered traps
and the broken land in wasteplots our playing field:
this was the world through which I learnt the world
and this the image for my vision of the world.

"Freedom!

"Freedom!
It's wonderful"
said the Ukrainian
on the train to Philadelphia.
"In the Ukraine
the Russians take away my freedom
but here I am free
to make sure the black man starves."

Amid the singing and the flowers

Amid the singing and the flowers
the candles and the prayers
another body goes—
while the choir soars—
out into the day.

What thrusts of loneliness

What thrusts of loneliness
or egotism
drove me to those phantasies?

I was invisible
had the power of flight
could shrink to the size of a mouse

So I waged my war
against pangs of desperateness
and a brutal intractable world

Orion's belt is out

Orion's belt is out;
the Hunter marches in a distant sky
recessed, as all stars are,
in this far dark clime:

the Twins hold their staunch alliance,
a starved Dog cowers in the grey,
somewhere, overhead, looms an alien and unknown
Plough:

only a planet's splash redeems the grimy murk,
that, and the faint blue silver luminous at a southern edge
where the City hurls its tinsel in the sky

—And the wonder of this open night
this almost unclouded winter sky
through the bare-wire strands of the naked trees
and lyric beauty running through the gloom.

Again the rain-silvered asphalt

Again the rain-silvered asphalt
a brilliant mirroring sheen,
brightness a shield for the pitted and rutted tar
now when an eastern brilliance blazes
an explosion of light on a freakish late-winter day:

Echo and image this, of an earlier transfiguring day,
long hope-haunted years hence
whose song-echo hoots down this tunnel of days

What other turning awaited?
what imagined ash-hearted delights?
what escapes, achievements, obscurity-calms?

Instead there is sorrow and pain and bitter defeat
and some small skirmishes triumphed;
for these trophies these prices could be paid once again:
one buys, for one's land, small hopes for much pain.

Again and in another way I triumph

Again and in another way I triumph
simply by this trust in their awareness
through the guard of distance
the cloak of space
the complex riverlock of circumstance
that impedes the flow of knowledge
and of facts.

Crossing Kabul to Samerkand

Crossing Kabul to Samerkand
en route to the Aral Sea
through the snowwastes of the Hindu Kush
Byzantine minarets appear
in a snowshower snow-mirage:

all magic;
or mystery, miracle, or grace;
and portent of strange unskeining designs
whose tracings marked those lighted days
of grey wall and blue stone and metal prison-bars
the colour of steel or night or shadow.

—and the air is filled with

—and the air is filled with
the ghosts of planes,
skeletons and shrapnel
in wild gyrations
and monsters lumber on
the bombing run

—and on the sea that raft
of boats
a sargasso of craft jam—
packed like bactrian spawn
in the sunlit fleececloud
sapphire day—

in such a day they went
to their terror and blast
men—gymnasts of terror and death
—no less than now
while the furry spiders
hunch in the City's streets

What am I in her eyes?

What am I in her eyes?
half-white, half-black—
chiefly half-white:
for her, with her own hang-ups,
coursers of darker hue,
mine is an alien image
a mixed ambivalent viscid thing
repellent; ambiguous,
in a less-hostile no-mans-land:
I am a puzzle, an irritant,
part-envied escaper, part pitied.

In my part of the world

In my part of the world,
In my part of Africa,
In my part of this continent of ours,
South Africa
(I am from South Africa)
we have a very simple greeting:
we say "Africa".
When we meet
 and when we part
we say "Africa".
And when we wish to express our brotherhood
our shared and common purpose
we say "Africa".
And when we wish to show our love
and declare our common will
we say "Africa".

In my part of Africa
we have a very simple greeting:
we say—
"Africa".

What is the soul of Africa?

What is the soul of Africa?
What is it?
Is there a soul of Africa?
Is it simply that we have
contrived to be what humans are
while everywhere humanity
was being deformed?
and in the new age of man
this lunatic unsublunary age
is it still valuable to be man?
to assert the old humanities?

Where the statues pose and attitudinize

Where the statues pose and attitudinize—
even the headless weathered ones—
on the garden terrace, overlooking the landscape,
weariness hangs,
droops over them in their centuries' stance
flap-dragging like limp airless flags—
thread-worn flags, their colours bleared and dim

And I weary with them, from their fourteenth-century
stance
and know they do not know the peace I seek:
("The secret", the Greeks said, "was not to be born",
and: "Call no man happy until he be dead".)
And the deepest attraction of death is its nothingness,
its promise of total unknowingness is bliss—
Then it will be nothing, but the promise is bliss.

To be restful like a potato, this is something
tho' growth or decay make tiresome demands—
birds pecking (eyes, hair, maid's nose) are nothing
are exterior, make no inner demands—
but better by far to be a stone;
blissfully insensible, oblivious, and better than that,
a stone, with totally insensible stoniness:

but to be a statue; this is too much—
up at Frascati villa, among the hills
where the sturdy-footmen olives cling to the hills,
in the splendour of Falconieri among its peers—
Aldobrandini and Mondragon heights;
here, in this opulence, still I shrink back—
to be a stone, not a statue, for this I yearn.

But Mister, you can't imagine

But Mister, you can't imagine
in this place
what elegancies, what intrigues
what exquisite cruelties
what opulence of voluptuousness
these quattrocento walls have seen

Rustle of silks, damasks and samite,
perfumes of wine and wild white roses
fetched from obscure and inaccessible heights

All swirl round me now
in my imaginings
and the mind reels
imagining the unimaginable.

A new guilt tension arises

A new guilt tension arises
a habit and craving
in collision with will and knowledge:
with an added conflict element—
the knowledge of disease—
to moral oppositions
based on forgotten, obscurely present resolves:
old synapses leap into existence anew
assert themselves in my body-labyrinth:
What now?
What new avenues open?
and what new griefs will not contend?

In England's green and pleasant land

In England's green and pleasant land
where "wogs" spit from the posters
and the swastika is a rallying sign
we will build a green and pleasant land:

When old Jerusalem is transformed
under an Occupation's Centurions
we must keep our vision, wage our faith
till old Jerusalem is transformed:

Bring me my bows of burning gold
to lance where the City's bullion snores
and erect me in indestructible desire
to bind with others in unquenchable rage
to exult in a new-made City's Great Fire.

What one is

What one is,
one is
gratefully,
being
what one
might not be

The golden afternoon drags

The golden afternoon drags,
lengthens:
in a placid cosy luster
of warm somnolence:
the day will grow longer
will extend

as we—craned-beak-bird flighted
eagle or snowgoose to St. Johns
away from Heathrow's forenoon
over an Atlantic's drowsy noon
to the flurries of snow-harried Manhattan.

So it was
once
in a golden August
when I winged this route
unconscious of my seasonal bliss
to the Hilton's luxury
and mango-golden Jamaica's lushness
accepting it all
lordly
as existent circumstance.

And I have done it again
and again

And now go to new terrain,
new snowy heights
and what new miserable uncertainties.

Had you lived

Had you lived
today we would have celebrated
the day of your birth:
but you are gone;
can we believe
your thought lives on
through those you taught
and your will to serve the world
in those who act,
as I do,
enriched by what you taught and thought?

They hanged him, I said dismissively

They hanged him, I said dismissively
having no other way to say he died
or that he was a dear friend
or that work wove us most intimately
in common tasks, ambitions, desires.
Now he is dead: and I dare not think
of the anguish that drove him to where he was
or the pain at their hands he must have faced
or how much he was racked by my distress:
now, it is still easiest to say, they hanged him,
dismissively.

There are no people left in my country

There are no people left in my country
only resolves;
only faceless ciphers for whom I assert
my concern:
solicitude
urges my action and my thought
and I cling to a program of release
stubbornly:
I do not dare to remember the multiple treacheries
cowardice,
the boots seeking a prisoner's gall,
the relatives
with lidded refuse-bins of knowledge behind their eyes:
because I cling to service for my people
with most desperate resolve
there are no people in my country
only faceless vulnerable wraiths
and insubstantial delicate resolves

The New York Times reports they say they are hurt

The New York Times reports they say they are hurt;
the telex carries news of an Australian decision;
in dorpies and plains in the Free State
the rugby-players writhe, running their hands
over the bruises of defeat in Britain,
West German friends renounce their neo-nazi posture,
a truncated tour mocks them with uncertainties
—everywhere the sportsmen draw in their robes
and withdraw, fearful of contamination,
while the foul ichor oozes from their wounds—
Indeed I flog fresh lashes across these thieves!
And they bleed.....

I will not climb the green hillside

I will not climb the green hillside
the white ducks ornament
nor saunter down to the shore
where agate waves coruscate

I will not gaze over blue valleys
to where far mountains hulk
shouldering against the sky
in burly unyieldingness

I will turn from Rome in the luminous dusk
and Tehran's blue and silver evenings,
only the seabirds wheeling from Algiers,
the evocative slopes below Carmel.....

At Manila airport

At Manila airport
transit passengers may not
look
at the
sunset:
beyond the glass doors
a man with a gun
orders you
"Inside"

At odd moments

At odd moments
my bullet scars will twinge:
when I am resting,
or when fatigue
is a continuous shriek in my brain:
and straightway
I am stiffened with resolve
and am aware of my task
almost with reverence
and with humility

Oh God

Oh God
the sight of these uniformed men
locusting the earth
for their fat harvesters
fills me with sadness
and sick anger and a horror-struck prescience
of the carnage to come

Fragrance of petunia after rain

Fragrance of petunia after rain
revives me
as the call to service
or high endeavour,
or the gangling grace
of the sapling silver-beech.

Swatches of brassy music

Swatches of brassy music
skein through the fug
smoke, liquor, sweat
laughter and erotic undulations
How shall we forgive them?

Men in the clutch of death
lust
in the last despairing gasp
of their animation
Why should they need forgiveness?

This night
in the endless light
of Robben Island
the men lie
with lidless eyes
and stare down the glaring corridor of time
with an open coffin at its end
and frantically scrape
at the bare smooth walls of unyielding knowledge
seeking some moss of comfort
some lichen-particle of hope
that shows there will be some change
some hint that freedom will arrive,
break through these walls of life-in-death
life-till-death
How will they forgive us?

A horror tumuluses in my brain
shoulders thought into incoherence;
oh men, oh managers
how can we dare to fail
how can we dare to choose to fail
How can we hope they will forgive us?

And after that?
will unforgiveness spoil the pleasant rasp
of the tepid beer we quaff
thirsty after the dance's gyrations?
Being cursed
will we sleep less sound
in the sticky languor of spent limbs
the flesh limply swollen with satiation
will that long billow of sigh
gusting through the prison corridors
disturb our sleeping ears?
will the sparse tears
unwillingly wrung
from contorted faces, mouths, eyes
of men desperately fighting for strength,
control,
will a large hot tear
dropping on concrete
wake us with its soundless splash?
or men mouthing bitter curses
or twisting their racked bodies
to try to minimize some area of the pain,
will these men rise up
to confront us
as our bodies flush and harden
with the slow tidal surge of lust
and make us limp with guilt?
or in the drowsy repletion
of our sexual aftermath
will their wraiths terrorise us
into wakefulness?

Swatches of brassy melody
skein the revelling air

Men under grip of death
lust for a final lust
in insensate assertion
of the guttering, soon-to-be-snuffed vital spark

In a gloom of dazzling perennial light
the prisoners yearn
outward
their longing visceral, vulnerable
like an extruded gut or glans

Schemers weave,
oblivious,
devious,
perhaps for unseen, not-to-be-whispered goals
and my protesting anger
storms at my eyes
with hot salt tears

We, not being mobilised
in will,
what can we hope for?
how can we get forgiveness
—if indeed it is sought or needed—?
and what will we achieve?

Somewhere in the mind
a stubborn kernel
—obligation, perhaps—
stubbornly persists.
The mind devises action.

I wander through your cozy aubergs, dreary cottages

I wander through your cozy aubergs, dreary cottages
and wonder at your cut-off unknowable streets
that end at the snow-low horizon:
guess at the gusts that shake your wintry branches,
shiver at the melancholy whiteness of new-fallen snow,

trample the sludge of accumulated guilts
and settle in the snow and mire, the brick and friends
of this soiled, weary, ineluctable being.

An Utrillo, possibly

Mounted
this thing became another thing—
this thing of browns and pinks and creams
of bulk and shapes
of passages and shadows—
masses acquired substance,
grew vibrant, set up subtle tensions
solids yearned towards solids;
one penetrated endlessly
to suspended horizons,
thrust at bulk
rubbed against masses
suspired in a timeless atmosphere
and in a great ocean of delicious pressures
swooned mind heart and flesh in a blissful surcease.

With my customary restraint

With my customary restraint
customary control
customary discretion
customary sagacity
customary wisdom
I will be silent:
knowing he is capable of spite
knowing he can do harm
damage
can injure the cause

I will be silent
and exercise my customary virtue:
        but it is a virtue I am doubtful of
                                   am suspicious of
            am sometimes contemptuous of:
Yet I will be silent
and perhaps applaud myself.

Lilac dusk

Lilac dusk,
and in the gathering dark
bulky hydrangeas nod and beckon
heliotrope,
outside the window.

You have your private griefs

You have your private griefs,
I mine:

Peace is not indifference
nor inaction;
but let us wall ourselves away from war:

Peace comes from inner certitude,
assurance about one's worth,
one's status, talents, labours;

and some security, surely,
about the nature of things,
directions;

ought we then not to care,
not to share a shared sorrow?

no virtue can transcend charity:
Peace without love is death,
the hollow ribcage of the cadaver

It is not size that makes mountains

It is not size that makes mountains
nor shape
but a certain earthsplendour quality,
a gathering of earthliness

There will be ample provision for the elite

There will ample provision for the elite
—and their servants—and their poodles—
in the planetary colonies
while we moulder to disintegration
(gas-masked) on the miasma
of an uninhabitable fug
or frizzle in the holocaust
of a thermonuclear fry.

Success cannot redeem despair

Success cannot redeem despair
nor can a catalogue of joys
recited, drown the wail of dismay:
I who can, squirming, turn in the dark
and find some magnitude of stars
—pinpricks to bar the dark's enfolding tide—
still catch at the edge of vision a flicker,

life's fragile pulse in a shadowed hollow at my wrist
discover I have no amulet against despair
no incantation to dismiss suicide
—what I have done—achieved—is no protection;
successes cannot save me from despair.

Sirens contrail the night air

Sirens contrail the night air:

Images of prisons around the world,
reports of torture, cries of pain
all strike me on a single sore
all focus on a total wound:

Isle of Shippey, Isle of Wight,
New Zealand and Australia
are places with a single name
—where I am they always are:

I go through the world with a literal scar,
their names are stitched into my flesh,
their mewedupness is my perennial ache,
their voice the texture of my air:

Sirens contrail the London air.

There will be others like you

There will be others like you
Perform your functions
Do the things you did so dearly
only never never
dearest you.

Oh Oh Oh Oh
The morning rises
now to potency

This is a land

This is a land
so vibrant and alive
that laughter will come bursting through
as imperious as the sun

and the spirit will survive
resilient as the soil.

What a continent this is

What a continent this is
that turns us all to jetsam
jettisons us, discards
seemingly all that are of worth.

With a certain ease

With a certain ease
—almost grace
a sign of assurance
in handling, notion, status

She called me
the most liberated man
she had ever known

The heart of man

The heart of man
has a secret centre
that flowers at a hint of beauty
—or all that aspires that to be.

Patriot I

The dust-devils of my fury
have not yet dervished on your nakedness
nor have I puked out anger
in a bile-bitter cataract
nor gusted private intimacies
in public obscenities to erode your stony calm:
but if in time I can endure no longer
the torturing of unrequitedness
and claw your contours with deliberate clumsiness,
I beg you to remember
such violence may be
perversion of frustrated tenderness.

The beauty of my land peers warily

The beauty of my land peers warily
through palisading trees on hilly slopes;
at night along the tree-fenced roads
I sense her presence pacing sinously
beyond the searching circle of the lights.
Exploring pools of soothing tepidness
I find the indrawn nerveless diffidence
of beauty fearing ravishment's delight;
I shiver at her self-defensive scorn
in chillness of aloofly soaring rocks—
But all of these my unwearying ardour mocks
when sunfire ignites the miles of rippling corn.

That people care

That people care
is more than money
their thoughts, their love, their prayers
this is what gives us strength

And when they praise
we are ashamed
of our complaints
our failure to endure

That people care
is more to us than weapons—
and that they share
our fight and its anxieties.

Stop

Stop.
I ask you to think for a moment
to think of pain
of hunger,
to think of people who are not free,
to think of death.

Stop.
Now.
Stop thinking of other things.
Think only of this—
of people dying
dying by the gun,
the boot,
the fist.
Think of them,
the people who are not free,
who will give their lives to be free.

Stop.
Now.
Think.
Now.
Then stand.
And lift your fist
and shout your anger
and your resolution;
Shout "Africa"
Three times
Now.
Africa.
Africa.
Africa.

Snarling, the great beast hurls through the dark

Snarling, the great beast hurls through the dark
arrows squatly over the ice-glazed track
thrusts, jarring for an instant, from the slithery earth
then soars; and arrogantly heels
shouldering sideways the still menace-full land
while the city throws up and lewdly unveils
naked, bejewelled, treasure-rope-pearls.

Beautiful Amsterdam,
Amsterdam so beautiful with all
her lights gaily decked
(O Amsterdam is tog so mooi met al haar liggies uitgetooi)

And we settle once more for the thundering flight—
one more wide range on a troubadour's earth.

And who can doubt that one day
we will set out and turn
and turn southward to that
one last journey for which we burn
and for which, as we journey
now, the heart yearns.

Profligate seminal milliards

Profligate seminal milliards
my ego's co-existences
yearn with theftuous motility
for acquisition of your other selves:
in your girdled scenic basin
facsimile of primal shores
they orgy (*luxe,calme et volupte*)
while I, lacustrine mallard,
brood, preen and nest.

Perhaps

Perhaps
all
poems
are simply
drafts

Over the ash and butts

Over the ash and butts
I move my hand
and brush another ghostly hand
and curse the world
in steady wordless monotone:
my guts wrench in wry awareness of this twisted world
in whose making we have had no hand.
Spirals of smoke unfurl
against my eyes in casual assault
ascending past me in the shadows
where I sit alone.

Oxen amuck stampede
and legislate
indifferently for our apartheid,
sever our hands
and every tenderness that clings:
they bleed
and shrivel desire's parched and parcelled lands
bar with lunatic-lucid hate
our twilight clumsied hands:

twisting like smoke-spiral strands
over absence's gulfs and streams
my heart still wings.

Love; the Struggle

Now the dawn's attack announces:
Light thrusts a thousand salients
To probe our dark's defences;
Limply now the curtains posture
Too unmobile to repulse
The day's outflanking pincers:
Stairs and bathroom creak life's permanent alarms
—Ah Love, unshoulder now my arms!

Now shuttered silk-lids open, shudder
At scar-shadows light brands everyday:
Look long, last, dismiss each other;
Lips sleep-curved in acquiescent parting
Tighten to resolve, farewell:
This is leaving, dying, is departing
Bereft our night, marauded of obliviousness to harms
—Ah Love, unshoulder now my arms!

Our tenuous luke-warmed pool of silence
Time's battery rocks and salvoes
From its niche in circumstance;

Conched, contrapuntal our concord
Day's breath wracks our peace,
Our dreams disrupt in blustery discord
Buckling to winds' capricious buffet we desert our calms
—Ah Love, unshoulder now my arms!

Era, anger summon fairplay
Unardent to the arduous strife
Heart, my dour heart turns from fairness;
Seas confront with seethe and trouble
Cries assail and thongs defy:
I gird from nestling to advance the struggle
A clinic dialectic titrates, dispells our charms
—Ah Love, unshoulder now my arms!

One kiss in turning, last-another,
Here, where spinal vacuum recalls,
Implant your charge before the smother;
From skin milk-soft, milk-mild-tender,
Confiding throat, accepting arm,
Pluck pulsing cadences: now end it.
Stars blear, nightbreaths fust and rasp: a clash, glint,
stench of arms!
Unshoulder, Love, unshoulder all my arms!

Nothing in my life

Nothing in my life
was more like a nightmare from "Der Prozess"

The bright surfaces
modern italianate colours
mosaicked pastel tiles
walls of glass
airy steel in networks, grilles
birdcages:

battens of fluorescents beating down
like bright walls of glass
and the chained prisoners running
shambling through grotesque three-legged races
through the long concrete quad
under the spanning concrete bridge
and the shadowy machine-gunned guard
and stumbling up the stairs
by the cool aquamarine walls—
the stairs cool under my fingers where I feel

Nothing in my life
more like a nightmare in "Der Prozess"

Robben Island Sequence

I

neonbright orange
vermilion
on the chopped broken slate
that gravelled the path and yard
bright orange was the red blood
freshly spilt where the prisoners had passed;

and bright red
pinkbright red and light
the blood on the light sand by the sea
the pale lightyellow seas and
in the light bright airy air
lightwoven, seawoven, spraywoven air
of sunlight by the beach where we worked:

where the bright blade-edges of the rocks
jutted like chisels from the squatting rocks
the keen fine edges whitening to thinness
from the lightbrown masses of the sunlit rocks,
washed around by swirls on rushing wave water,
lightgreen or colourless, transparent with a hint of light:

on the sharp pale whitening edges
our blood showed light and pink,
our gashed soles winced from the fine barely felt slashes,
that lacerated afterwards:
the bloody flow
thinned to thin pink strings dangling
as we hobbled through the wet clinging sands
or we discovered surprised
in some quiet backwater pool
the thick flow of blood uncoiling
from a skein to thick dark red strands.

The menace of that bright day was clear as the blade
of a knife;
from the blade edges of the rocks,
from the piercing brilliance of the day,
the incisive thrust of the clear air into the lungs
the salt-stinging brightness of sky and light on the eyes:
from the clear image, bronze-sharp lines of Kleynhans
laughing
khaki-ed, uniformed, with his foot on the neck of the
convict who had fallen,
holding his head under water in the pool where he had
fallen
while the man thrashed helplessly
and the bubbles gurgled
and the air glinted dully on lethal gunbutts,
the day was brilliant with the threat of death.

II

sitting on the damp sand
in sand-powdered windpuff,
the treetops still grey in the early morning air
and dew still hanging tree-high,
to come to the beginning of the day
and small barely-conscious illicit greetings
to settle to a shape of mind, of thought,
and inhabit a body to its extremities:
to be a prisoner, a political victim,
to be a some-time fighter, to endure—
find reserves of good cheer, of composure
while the wind rippled the tight skin forming on the
cooling porridge
and sandspray dropped by windgusts depressed it:
to begin, at the beginning of a day, to be a person
and take and hold a shape to last for this one day.....

(afterwards the old lags came along
with their favourite warders, to select
the young prisoners who had caught their eye,
so that these could be assigned to their span)

III

some mornings we lined up for "hospital"
—it meant mostly getting castor oil—
but what a varied bunch we were!
for all had injuries—but in such variety
split heads; smashed ankles, arms;
cut feet in bandages, or torn and bloodied legs:
some, under uniform, wore their mass of bruises
but what a bruised and broken motley lot we were!

It is the men

It is the men
who assert man's common worth
most plangently
who are the proudest boast
of most men's lands:

but we have no such heroes
no such boasts:
those who attempt it are our private shames
—or else efficiently suppressed.

Is it so terrible that you should love another

Is it so terrible that you should love another
and is it wholly true that you no longer retain
even a tiny particle—a shred or ravelling
of love for me
Did you not say that there would always be
some of your heart for me.

This seems a new Passion, a small Gethsemane, for me.
Shall I go for consoling to your letters?
They might bring some sanity—
recalling my endeavours to shake you from me.

In Teheran

In Teheran
where I was born
or where I've been
Or where I belong

—it's all one
for it's all one world
and everywhere
it's all one place.....

How then do I justify
this stubborn single-track anxiety
for this one place?
this sad, mad, silly, pitiable concern?

Kingston on Thames to Kingston, Jamaica
Tuskegee to Teheran,
Stockholm to Seattle
Dakar to Dar es Salaam:
Oslo to the Cape.....

Land it is not.
Not when Carmel and Las Palmas call.
Nor climate, town nor family.
Nor history or geography.

In a broad-brimmed black hat

In a broad-brimmed black hat
over his eyes a black mask
enormous shoulders hunched in his black coat
a black man in the bathroom,
Honey, waits.
Blots out white walls
and white bathroom tiles
the pale light from the plastic curtains
and the mirror's false white dimensions.
Waits.

I remember the simple practicality of your reminiscences

I remember the simple practicality of your reminiscences
and sneer at the orgasmic adulation
with which beautiful poetesses write your elegies,
remember those great grotesque cigars—
(fellatio, or sexual surrogates)
the display of bare manly flesh,
recall

the
confessions
of
Lawrence
in the
desert
and
know
how
much
can be
meretricious
and falsified.

But still
you
walked
through the
Sierra Maestra
like a
giant
and endured
the petty hardships
and great
strain;
And asthma
wracked you
from the Granma time
that petty humbling
and neurotic affliction
that revealed an integral defect,

some human flaw
that made you kin
with weakest humanity.

I do not fear your loss now

I do not fear your loss now
but when I face the absolute tests
how shall I fare without your central love?
This is what, without reproach, I fear.

When you return there will be nothing new

When you return there will be nothing new
not even in the manner of our meeting
nor in the infinite words of greeting
for I have spent my thoughts on you
exhausted every shade of meaning
imagined every motion of your breath
(except the true, it stilled in death)
and whether sleeping or daydreaming
rehearse our every varied stance
explore each phrase's fine nuance
and know that I shall answer with assent
though now I lie exhausted, jaded, spent.

I can understand

I can understand
how the shopgirls lust
to spreadeagle themselves
before such brute efficiency:
even the dust
of my wounded land
endures their boots
submissively

Hold me, my dear, hold me

Hold me, my dear, hold me:
while winds gather for seething
and engines rev to charge,
across all these miles
of taut aching dark
let me be assured of this—
amid the buffets and the metal
is still a possible tenderness.

Having fled, I display a fugitive's jealousy

Having fled, I display a fugitive's jealousy,
regard my heart suspiciously
caution it against seduction by another's charms
chafe against those who criticise
or praise too lavishly
and those who, being with you
are indifferent, blind,
or take too much delight in you

Tenement Balcony

From here I see the shanties
and the indomitable trees:
and standing on the rubble of a thousand I's
I see these trees and far clear skies.

For the children

For the children
for whom the flesh is not yet a burden
this is not an occasion for celebration
in quite this way at all:

but for us who know
just how massive was the cost
of adopting the garb of flesh
and the travail it entails

and who have plummetted
through the range of bestiality
that man is capable of
this transcendant act
of God assuming man's pathetic flesh
is something to be grateful for

Even though you weave her

Even though you weave her
with energetic quills
Medea-robes of flames
and thus contrive to smother
motion, speech and shame
yet in this clash of wills
I'll not consent to leave her
nor ever cease to love her
and herein lies my brute resistance.

Dear God

Dear God
get me out of here:
let me go somewhere else
where I can fight the evil
which surrounds me here
and which I am forbidden to fight
—but do not take from me my anger
my indignation at injustice
so that I may continue to burn
to right it or destroy.

Oh I know
I have asked for this before
in other predicaments
and found myself most wildly involved

But if it be possible
and conformable to your will
dear God,
get me out of here.

Cemeteries, it seems, remain the same

Cemeteries, it seems, remain the same
through centuries: vainly the creepers forge
insipid fetters for still greying stone,

stubbly-anaemic grasses wilt despite
their luscious breast-and-buttock compost
and senescence of tree and headstone merge

into the staled and melancholy rule
of faded but imperishably stubborn love
more durable than death or crumbled flesh.

Thus, surely, tyrannies decay
while spirit and affections still endure:
celled-in or isolated, banned from speech

and shadowed by pendant manacles
the spirit's aspirations will survive these things
spirit, and our unquenchable love of land

In Memoriam: I.A.H.

Being dead
it does not matter
how guilty or innocent he died

we are free to speak
though because he chose not to speak
he died.

Being dead
it does not matter
how well or ill he died

—now they can touch him not
though it was under their pulping boots
he died.

Yet the living
for whom he put out tendrils of self
must live miasma-ed by his death

and the flowers he put forth for them
are now pale wreaths of terror
with the sick-sweet smell of death.

Being dead
we might pay him tribute
but it was for the living he died

and we must content ourselves in saying
'it was for our cause he died'
and inwardly know for what cause he died.

*Imam Abdulla Haroun; 'found dead of natural causes' in his cell in Cape Town, after being held without trial for four months by the Secret Police.

At the apex of these sumptuous columns

At the apex of these sumptuous columns
lurks the secret mystery
the bunching of tissue hirsuted
scented pungently
aura-ed in dizzying waves
radiating a tremoring magic
radiant heat pulsing like blushes
and secret tremulous pulses
quivering in expectance of rude embrace
—a must of vinous swirls
whelming blood, brain and sight

Penelope

At Ithaca, weaving at shroud or snood
while he, nostalgically frenzied, hogged
your Circe-image in the aphrodisiac air
imagination must have shuttled between bed and bier
the spindle-phallus swelling in your fashioning hand
until an ichor trickle from the tissue seeped.
Your psyche must have soared on Eros wings
or plummetted like Icarus to wine's dark seas.

We survive, if nothing else remains

We survive, if nothing else remains
in assurance of affliction,
pains:
for you and I,
by this infliction
each on each
of private agony,
the certainty of suffering,
know
something of the heart's immortality:
and though
we die each day
we know too,
in the heart of each,
remembrance survives—
this pain we suffer
we inflict
we cherish and enjoy,
knowing that in this way
somehow
we keep alive
something of the love we knew.

Five Minutes to Midnight

For B.B.K.

Anger prowls in the tranquil dusk
Where milkwhite and blue the moonlight glows
On the opal glimmer of a dreaming breast
Rising and falling as the sweet air flows

When strikes the tiger? Ah, who knows?

Open the breast to the tiger's thrust
Where moonwhite and naked the soft flesh glows
Blue where the bloodstream's brooklets twist
Warming the cool bed's tombwhite clothes

When drinks the tiger? Ah, who knows?

Open the breast to the whispering air
Like caressing endearment it wavelike flows
But the air is foul with a beastlike breath
Whitehot and wild with a milliard woes

When leaps the tiger? Ah, who knows?

Closed is the breast to a gale of pleas
Closed to the beat of the tear-filled seas
(Closed is the door through which terror flees)
Unheeded the stream of blood-guilt flows

When feeds the tiger? Ah, who knows?

Although you need not care

Although you need not care
and nothing can detract
from the beatific bliss of heaven
yet, obscurely, I can sadden
or increase your joy:

and I can make you happy
and you rejoice
when others give me happiness.

Age and anguish yield a harvest

Age and anguish yield a harvest
star-precious as the lilts of youth
inhabit an arctic of perennial grief
For those who never see the sun
the cold is a familiar
and dark the normal habitat
The barnacles of grief acquire patinas
They yield their own
deceptive light
our hearts become
inured to dying.

The mountain fastnesses

The mountain fastnesses,
the blank flat hostility of the plains
the charnel underground
seamed and ribbed with bones,
the smog, smear, smother of the city—
dust and assaulting grime

My fortress, my retreat
bastion against my enemies
base for my evanescent security

Where I am, scared rabbit, everywhere assailed.

from *China Poems*

Dennis Brutus

from China Poems

The road from Peking Airport

Avenues of trees
for miles:
cicadas singing.

Beyond the trees

Beyond the trees
the limitless
horizon.

The tree in the Emperor's Garden

The tree in the Emperor's Garden
will not accept
the discipline of marble.

*(The Forbidden City—now the
Peoples' Palace of Leisure.)*

On the roofs

On the roofs
of the ruined palaces of Emperors
imperial lions snarl
at the empty air.

(In the Forbidden City.)

Over the Bridge of Golden Water

Over the Bridge of Golden Water
through the Gate of Heavenly Peace
in the Forbidden City
is the Peoples' Palace of Leisure.

(At a Festival of Childrens' Dances
in the Peoples' Palace of Leisure,
once the Forbidden City, children
gave me a bunch of paper flowers.
I composed and recited this poem,
partly as an expression of my
appreciation.)

Poplar

1.

A tall slender poplar
with sun-dappled leaves:
a comparison
is a generous, tender, compliment.

2.

His poplar's beauty
was cut down;
sad felicity.

At the Long Wall

At the Long Wall:
a soldier
holding a flower.

Seeing the peaks

Seeing the peaks
they had to conquer
lost in the mists
their spirits must have quailed:
but a sense of the intimacy
between humankind and earth
kept them strong.

A fern

A fern
can seize the artist
with its beauty.

Earthworks covered with moss

Earthworks covered with moss.
an empty goldfish bowl.
a piglet, a melon.

(A People's Commune.)

China

China:
landscape, but not with figures;
people.

The barges clamorous on the river

The barges clamorous on the river,
the men, in pairs, rhythmically leaning on their poles:
storied city of crime, plunder and intrigue—
now the people reconstruct.

(Recited at a Banquet, Shanghai Mansions
—on the Headquarters of the Japanese
Army of Occupation.)

Do all old men feel thus?

Do all old men feel thus?
Youth thrusting truculently,
young men, young women
aswirl in sensual vitality
advancing tidally;
we shrivel at the center
curl and wither with brittle edges.

The lust of the eyes

The lust of the eyes
is a cobra, hooded;
in prison the serpent drowses.

(Friendship Hotel, Peking)

I have commuted between the world's capitals

I have commuted between the world's capitals:
travel is no longer an achievement;
I must begin to do meaningful things.

The mirror serves

The mirror serves:
the viewer
sets the angle.

Not in my hands

Not in my hands
is the clay
of my life

from Strains

from Strains

Sabotage, 1962

Here, thunderheads rear in the night
dominating the awed quiet sky;
on the quiet-breathing plains
fractured metals shriek abandoned wails;
my country, an ignorantly timid bride
winces, tenses for the shattering releasing tide.

At night

At night
on the smooth grey concrete of my cell
I heard the enormous roar of the surf
and saw in my mind's eye
the great white wall of spray rising
like a sheet of shattering glass
where the surge broke
on the shore and rocks and barbed wire
and going to the shed
in hope of a visitor
I greeted the great cypresses
green and black
dreaming in their poised serenity
in the limpid stillness of the brilliant afternoon
gracious as an Umbrian Raphael landscape
but more brilliant and more sharp.

The year of the giant

The year of the giant.
The year of the dragon.
The year of the thin lizard,
Death.

It may be I will go
the way he went.
Who cares.
To me it is all one.
To me,
but not to others.
We shall see.

Our allies are exiles

Our allies are exiles
dark flames beating
on the rim of a dark world

they prowl and howl
like gaunt wolves
at the edge of the besieged clearing

and a thin wail
is picked up in the raucous air
of the wailing, waiting ghetto.

Spare La Guma
thin with intentness
worn to a point of pursuit

and flamboyant Nkosi
mannered with art
and querulous urging

Brutus scuffed with travail
lugging his crumpled sac
of tenderness turned to pain

and Cosmo and the many others
vibrant and willing
with artistry deployed to purpose

sage-seeming Zeke
all unrest churned
to containment and resolve

and that best-singing
bullocking, choiring KAN
silent
his notes stopped by clay and vomit
now a penumbra,
a spectral flame
burning like an ideal
on the horizon of our awareness
great victim
of the world's racist plague.

Our allies are exiles
to their earth unreturnable
or corpses that rot in alien earth

Africa's jacaranda dusk

Africa's jacaranda dusk
descends on Ibadan;
the trees poise
against the grey sky
while the red earth glows:

this is my sustenance;
the spirit is refreshed
the flesh renewed
while the sun smoulders
and the trees tower.

One red leaf

One red leaf
the first of its clan
dances by my window
while winter growls
in the throat of the lake.

Anticipations of disaster

Anticipations of disaster
shadow my calendar of days
while I chart my traverse
on stubborn assumptions of sun. . .

Kali was the destroyer

Kali was the destroyer;
also, somehow, the loved-one:
Reason, of course, could not
explicate the conflict;
nor I, though I know it to be true.

As a ghost in the starlight.
Sun Tzu: The Art of War

Moving intangibly
like a ghost in the starlight
he is obscure:
his target is the mind of the enemy.

And now there is one more
and the ranks swell,
the ghosts of glorious voices
stilled:

but their voices move people,
long palisades arise.
brief bright metallic glints
flash:

and listen:
across the sleeping veld,
over the bush and shadowed valleys
comes a long resolute roar.

World, I surrender you

World, I surrender you:
ignore me: let me be:
let me disown and disclaim you,
you are too much for me
let me abdicate,
be absolved of you:

the hands of demands pluck at me
tear like piranhas my naked flesh,
stripping me down to the bone

Saffron and orange and blood

Saffron and orange and blood
like this
seeped into the sky on other dawns
riding the army truck to prison
looking through bars at the island's day:

and so many since:
red anger gushes through my brain
in a bloodstream.
O when will my comrades stir
O when will their furious speech
turn to grim and unswervable resolve?

From Shannon

At dawn
through patches of woolly cloud
I descend over the Lake District
—smoke-greys, slate-blues—
where Wordsworth, Coleridge and other poets walked:
words that I loved—
catching their lilt, their melodic intonation:
but words that will not work
nor free the men who crouch
over the piles of slate
and swing grey hammers
with their broken hands.

Sharpeville

What is important
about Sharpeville
is not that seventy died:
nor even that they were shot in the back
retreating, unarmed, defenceless

and certainly not
the heavy calibre slug
that tore through a mother's back
and ripped through the child in her arms
killing it

Remember Sharpeville
bullet-in-the-back day

Because it epitomized oppression
and the nature of society
more clearly than anything else;
it was the classic event

Nowhere is racial dominance
more clearly defined
nowhere the will to oppress
more clearly demonstrated

what the world whispers
apartheid declares with snarling guns
the blood the rich lust after
South Africa spills in the dust

Remember Sharpeville
Remember bullet-in-the-back day

And remember the unquenchable will for freedom
Remember the dead
and be glad

For Frank Teruggi

A single rose
a single candle
a black coffin
a few mourners
weeping:

for the unsung brave
who sing in the dark
who defy the colonels
and who know
a new world stirs.

*No matter for history**

He lived,
he died:
no matter for history.

Through pain-cataracted eyes,
the legendary crab
pincering his viscera
he saw the ruins of his land
falling, falling
like debris after an explosion,
tiles scattering from a bombed house.

He lived;
no matter for history,
no fit matter to chronicle;

he watched his life's work
splinter like a crushed egg

no matter;

in death
the generals festered over him
like blowflies

his voice
sings on,
sings men to resistance,
to hope, to life;

Neruda is dead;
no matter.

*Pablo Neruda: *I lived: no matter for history.*

from *South African Voices*

from **South African Voices**

Sequence for South Africa

1.

Golden oaks and jacarandas
flowering:
exquisite images
to wrench my heart.

2.

Each day, each hour
is not painful,
exile is not amputation,
there is no bleeding wound
no torn flesh and severed nerves;
the secret is clamping down
holding the lid of awareness tight shut—
sealing in the acrid searing stench
that scalds the eyes,
swallows up the breath
and fixes the brain in a wail—
until some thoughtless questioner
pries the sealed lid loose;

I can exclude awareness of exile
until someone calls me one.

3.

The agony returns;
after a crisis, delirium,
surcease and aftermath;
my heart knows an exhausted calm,
catharsis brings forgetfulness
but
with recovery, resilience
the agony returns.

4.

At night
to put myself to sleep
I play alphabet games
but something reminds me of you
and I cry out
and am wakened.

5.

I have been bedded
in London and Paris
Amsterdam and Rotterdam,
in Munich and Frankfort
Warsaw and Rome—
and still my heart cries out for home!

6.

Exile
is the reproach
of beauty
in a foreign landscape,
vaguely familiar
because it echoes
remembered beauty.

On the Coming Victory

Behind the dark hills
the spears of dawn advance;
shadows and cobweb mists
shrink into gullies, ravines,
holes in the ground:
the terrible ghosts
pale, before terror, to nothingness;
the fieldflowers, drenched and bowed
lift with the coming light:
the long night lumbers grudgingly
into the past.

I am a rebel and freedom is my cause

I am a rebel and freedom is my cause:
Many of you have fought similar struggles
therefore you must join my cause:
My cause is a dream of freedom
and you must help me make my dream reality:
For why should I not dream and hope?
Is not revolution making reality of hopes?
Let us work together that my dream may be fulfilled
that I may return with my people out of exile
to live in one democracy in peace.
Is not my dream a noble one
worthy to stand beside freedom struggles everywhere?

For Anyan

Passionate intellection
made me a virtuoso
of dazzling bravura:
thousands of facets of the world
coruscated as thoughts, shapes, sounds;
my mind, peacock-eyed,

my ears, planetree responsive
and my tongue, armadillo-voracious
for talismanic words,
sang, spoke, saw, made magic:
Love, your love made me a poet.

The sunset flush

The sunset flush
bright gold and rose
dying over grey Manhattan
does not move me

and as we lunge
roaring past sapphire lights
breasting a tide of dusk
my mind is easy

Death may come
on this as on any other flight
and find me untroubled
except for the loss of joy
you promise me.

I will not agonize over you

I will not agonize over you:

when my heartbeats' steady pulses
surge to an impulse to ejaculate your name
(my tongue moves to a familiar flicker)

or my muscles' tensing and thrust
mount through my body till my lips pout
shaping kisses for your imagined mouth

when all my being remembers
and exclaims my love for you—
I will be steadfast and firm,
calmly observe and quiet my mind.

I will not agonize over you.